MW00477292

T H E   W A Y

DEMON ANGELS

TRICK, TRAP,
· A N D ·
TRAMPLE

BY
JACK W. HAYFORD

THE WAY DEMON ANGELS TRICK, TRAP, AND TRAMPLE

Published by Living Way Ministries
14300 Sherman Way
Van Nuys, CA (USA) 91405-2499
(818) 779-8400 • (800) 776-8180

ISBN 0-916847-17-9
Printed in the United States of America

TABLE OF CONTENTS

Please note: This book (The Way Demon Angels Trick, Trap, and Trample) is an editorial adaptation which will explain any difference you may find from Pastor Jack Hayford's usual written style. Care was taken to seek to retain the dynamic of his message as it was originally delivered.

But
there are
other angels
who
are not
our friends
—*they are our foes.*

DEMON ANGELS

TRICK, TRAP,

· A N D ·

TRAMPLE

Today there is an increasing interest in angels. I am not addressing the subject of angels because it is a current fad. However, I am addressing it because of my deep concern for people who miss God's intended purpose for their lives in their search for what they perceive as spiritual reality.

Angels are real beings, created by God. Good angels are intelligent beings commissioned by God in the interest of those who have opened to His saving grace. These angels are friends who speak a message that comes from God. And that message from God is intended to help us realize our destiny and His ultimate goal for us.

But there are other angels who are not our friends—they are our foes.

There is a vast difference between the true and faithful angels and the ones who are in the darkness and will lead you down a dark path. It is important for you to discern the difference, so you can relate to angels in a way that avoids becoming destructive to you.

It is my desire that people have truthful insights about angels; so they might experience the beauty of the real truth from God that blesses us and makes us fruitful. My heart aches for those who try to find the answer to the knotty web of their problems from a source that ultimately ends up bringing them confusion and destruction. I want to discuss how to avoid being tricked, trapped, and trampled by fallen angels.

God has not consigned us to superstition, magic signs, or "secret ways" to get in touch with Him. He has given us His Word, the Bible, as our ultimate "Source-book" to plainly reveal His heart and His ways. The Bible speaks with accuracy and practicality on many aspects of life—including angels.

It is important for us to study the Bible in order to get a clear perspective on angels—their reality, their history, their destiny, and the difference between the good and evil ones. Please note the following seven biblical facts about angels. I encourage you to study these facts and the Scripture references given with them. I believe a solid, biblical framework is essential for us as we begin our study on the fallen angels.

BIBLICAL TRUTHS ABOUT ANGELS

1. God Himself is the Creator of the angels, and as God, Christ is their Maker and Lord above all the angelic host (Genesis 2:1; Ephesians 3:9; Colossians 1:16).

2. Angels were created before and separate from humans. They were there at the creation of the earth and the present order of things (Job 38:1,4,7).

3. Angels were created with a free will and given supernatural strength and intelligence to serve God's will and purpose (Psalm 104:4; 103:20-21).

4. By reason of pride, a leading angel attempted to usurp God's throne. He was banished to earth with those angels who joined his

rebellion (Isaiah 14:12-15;
Revelation 12:3-4, 9).

5. In their hate and defiance of God, these evil
    angels seek to deceive humans and subtly
    lead them away from God and His love
    shown to us in Jesus Christ (John 8:44;
    2 Corinthians 11:13-15).

6. The fact that this rebellion and deception
    exists calls us to discernment and holy resis-
    tance (Ephesians 6:10-13).

7. Amid this conflict, God in His grace has
    assigned faithful angels to guard those
    humans who seek His ways (Psalm 34:7;
    Psalm 91:11-12; Hebrews 1:14).

OUR FASCINATION WITH ANGELS

There are a number of reasons why I believe there is such a resurgent interest in angels today.

First of all, many people are reacting to the materialistic values of society which have devalued their personhood. People have concluded, "I am *not* just a bundle of chemicals, and I am *not* just a person driven by animal energies. There's more to me than that: there's another part of me that is real and durable."

Our society has tried to play God by "removing" Him, but we are coming to recognize that there is more to life than that which can be seen. A person will say, "Well there must be something, but I've already said, 'there is no God' and 'I don't really want Him that much.' Besides, who knows if He exists? So there must be something more.

I sense these energies and dynamisms. How can I get in touch with something of the paranormal, the supernatural, or the other side, whatever there may be?"

In that human pursuit, "angels" come into play. And angels become subject to almost any definition! For example, for one person, an angel could be someone who helped finance a project of theirs. To another, an angel could be a "force" that seems to be on their side, or it could be a "power" referred to in a remarkable experience. For some people, an angel is a "being" they believe they have come in contact with, but they don't know how to explain or relate to it.

Many people are involved in a quest for divine guidance. There is a secret cry for hope in their hearts. They say to themselves, "If there is another realm, a spiritual realm, how can I get in touch with it? What help can I find?"

Friend, that help is available, and it does come from the invisible realm. There is a living God who created us; He is wiser than all, more powerful than all, and has offered all of His resource and life to us. He wants to bless, lead, and direct us. And He's given us His handbook—the Bible—to say, "Here's the way it works!"

The Bible is not passé, and it really isn't

heavy-handed. People often take a couple of verses out of context and get upset because it seems like there's only judgment, correction, and punishment in the Bible. They say, "Well, I can't handle a God who is like that." What they are really saying is: "I can't handle a me that doesn't want to live with being accountable to God, because I've done things that aren't worthy of being a creature of God. I want off the hook." And God says, "I'm holding you to it"; but He doesn't hold us to responsibility mercilessly. He says, "I want you to receive of My mercy, *then* align with My way." But we want to find our own way. We are so tempted and taunted in that direction that consequently we turn another way.

People are looking for some type of divine guidance, some help, some source of the supernatural. In their quest, there comes a vulnerability to angels—but not the good ones! (The idea that some angels are evil is contrary to what is commonly believed.)

We are not to seek out angels. **The Bible says that we are to establish a relationship with God; and *He* will take care of appointing the angels to take care of us**. Our business isn't to traffic in angels, but some people do. Once people start trafficking in angels, they don't recognize that (having departed from looking to the Lord) they are looking to man's way and wisdom.

In reality, these people are trafficking in evil angels, deceiving angels…devils who have chosen to follow in the wake and the trail of the devil—the arch enemy of all that is God's purpose.

Many people have become entangled and lost in what is a global-wide struggle for human allegiance. God offers His love, which is why He doesn't stamp out everything evil. If He did…people who are walking in their own way wouldn't have a chance to get back to Him. But evil persists and pursues; and, with passion, evil seduces and convinces a vast host of people to "do it your own way."

A DIVINE
WARNING
AGAINST
A DEVILISH
REALITY

The Bible talks about what happens when people resort to fallen angels. When God gives a warning, He is not hinting, "I'm going to get even with you if you do these things." He wants to prevent you from participating in a practice that will bring you to a sad and destructive end.

The passage of Scripture we are about to read is a prophecy that was given nearly twenty-seven hundred years ago. This passage of Scripture speaks with such severe warning that every ear should hear with wisdom and understanding.

In this passage, Isaiah the prophet spoke to a people (not unlike our own culture) who were interested in the supernatural because they wanted answers for their lives. The fact that our society has advanced in years from their society does not change the truth or relevance of Isaiah's message. It is as relevant today as it was then.

If there is a fundamental arrogance to our humanity and culture, it is the supposition that—because we have a different technology, because the cut of our clothes is different, because we can put the Hubble telescope in outer space and study some of the developments of the far reaches of our galaxy—there must be something of a particular advancement in us as people. The technological advancement really is short shrift compared to the real essence of the eternal nature of our being. When you come to that part of us, we are all the same: people have similar questions and problems. No matter what century people happen to live in, their symptoms of deep spiritual hunger draw their interest to angels.

Our Bible text is Isaiah 47:8-14. In this passage, people were resorting to three categories of fallen angels.

8 *"Therefore hear this now, you who are given to pleasures, who dwell securely, who say in your heart, 'I am, and there is no one else besides me; I shall not sit as a widow, nor shall I know the loss of children';*

9 *But these two things shall come to you in a moment, in one day: the loss of children, and widowhood. They shall come upon you in*

their fullness because of the multitude of your
sorceries, for the great abundance of your
enchantments.

10 *For you have trusted in your wickedness; you*
have said, 'No one sees me'; your wisdom and
your knowledge have warped you; and you
have said in your heart, 'I am, and there is no
one else besides me.'

11 *Therefore evil shall come upon you; you shall*
not know from where it arises. And trouble
shall fall upon you; you will not be able to put
it off. And desolation shall come upon you
suddenly, which you shall not know.

12 *Stand now with your enchantments and the*
multitude of your sorceries, in which you have
labored from your youth—perhaps you will be
able to profit, perhaps you will prevail.

13 *You are wearied in the multitude of your*
counsels; let now the astrologers, the stargazers,
and the monthly prognosticators stand up and
save you from what shall come upon you.

14 *Behold, they shall be as stubble, the fire shall*
burn them; they shall not deliver themselves
from the power of the flame; it shall not be a
coal to be warmed by, nor a fire to sit before!"

There are a legion of problems that arise
when people resort to fallen angels. The point of
resort is at the end of verses 9 and 12: *"Because of
the multitude of your sorceries…the great abun-*

dance of your enchantments. …Stand now with your enchantments and the multitude of your sorceries." This category has to do with what is in verse 13, *"You are wearied in the multitude of your counsels"* [or counselors]. Sorcerers, enchantments, psychic counselors, mediums, diviners, soothsayers, divination—all these involve the realm of **psychic counsel**.

Psychic counsel is administered by people who gain information and "wisdom" through submission of themselves to the realm of the fallen angelic—which is the demonic realm. By trafficking in demons they become mediators between fallen angels and human beings who need and want help spiritually. Fallen angels are very willing to cooperate with any human instrument they can find who will assist them in luring, seducing, confusing, and finally damning people who seek their counsel rather than God's. Later we will explore the reasons why psychics sometimes seem to know as much as they do.

A second category of fallen angels mentioned in Isaiah 47 is the category of **"I am."** We read about it in the middle of verse 8. Notice the phrase that says, *"I am, and there is no one else besides me."* This is repeated at the end of verse 10, *"I am, and there is no one else besides me."*

When I talk about the angel of "I am," I am

not referring to the positive worth that comes when a person is in right relationship with God. God wants us to be restored to a sense of personal worth and esteem. He wants us to come to Him and let Him bring us to a place of discovery of who we are and what we are about. As we come to that place, we can say, "Lord, thank You for what You made me to be." We find our source of worth, value, and esteem in Him. As we do that, we find what it means to have God on our side—which essentially is our coming on His side. I like those words of Lincoln long ago. When asked, "Do you think God is on your side?" Lincoln replied, "I'm not so concerned as to whether God is on my side. I just want to be sure I'm on His side." I want to get on God's side and be on the good side of God...it's possible for us to be exactly that.

I trust I have made it clear that when I talk about the angel of "I am," I'm not referring to the value God lovingly ascribes to us. I am talking about a being who has fallen away from God and whose behavior is rooted in an arrogant attitude that says, "I am, and there is none beside me."

The third type of fallen angels mentioned in this passage is in verse 13: *"Let now the astrologers, the stargazers, and the monthly prognosticators stand up and save you."* This verse tells us that there are people who have been resorting to those who take their **guidance from the stars**.

So this passage of Isaiah deals with these three categories of fallen angels that seduce people:
1. the angel of psychic counsel;
2. the angel of "I am"; and
3. the angel of the stars.

WHAT
HAPPENS
WHEN
PEOPLE
SEEK
"THEIR WAY"

Before I elaborate on each of the three categories of fallen angels; I want you to notice the problem that results when people say, "I'll not have the way of the Lord or the way of His Word. I want to do it my way. I've got to have some spiritual counsel because I believe that I'm a spiritual being" And so they start seeking. This seeking could be through tabloid literature. It could be through medical reports of people who "die" on the operating table but are revived and later talk about phenomenal things that happened while they were gone. Whatever the type of unusual phenomenon, if you interpret it on the basis of human wisdom rather than the wisdom of God—you are accepting what the Bible calls the wisdom of this world which is earthly, sensual, and devilish.

This kind of wisdom starts out as good, old, practical human wisdom, earthly. Then it becomes sensual; which means that at some point in your life it begins to control you at a sensory level. Then you begin to respond to this sensual appeal. **No one says, "I want a demon." Instead they say, "I would like my own angel." But what they get is a demon.** This is an important distinction; because once this takes place, the next stage will be to lure you to some point of sensuality. It can be sexual sensuality. It can be habitual sexuality. It can be attitudinal. It can be any number of things from arrogance and smugness, to anger you can't control, to things that will end at who knows where.

Let's look again at the text in Isaiah 47:9. *"But these two things shall come to you in a moment, in one day: the loss of children, and widowhood."* God is not saying here, "I'm going to beat up on your family. I'm going to kill your husband and your kids." God is not in the murdering business. The Bible says that it is the thief (the devil) who comes to steal and to kill and to destroy (John 10:10). I wish I could push a wonderful button in heaven and immediately restore every broken home that I have ever dealt with in pastoral work. Homes that were broken because the people submitted themselves to forces that they thought were just innocent or curious explorations; but these explorations became bondage and finally destroyed their family relationships.

In verse 11 it says, *"Therefore evil shall come upon you; you shall not know from where it arises."* This coming of evil does not mean a person is suddenly encountered by a phantom or an eighteen-foot tall demon. Rather, it means that by a person's exposure to these things the spirits will "come upon": in other words, there comes a surrounding sense of presence. Satan is wise enough to "come upon" people in a seductive way that at first seems innocent, desirable, and worthy.

Satan is not foolish. If he came on with all the ferocity of his intent, he wouldn't have any takers. **But he comes first as an angel of light.** This seems so good and feels so right that a person doesn't even suspect where it's coming from. God says that when you do this, you don't realize that you have opened yourself to another realm. You don't know where it's coming from; but it's not coming from heaven, because you have sought your own counsels. You have said, "I am, and there is none besides me." And you have sought the counsel of man and his limited wisdom. No matter how beautifully packaged the offer of psychic counsel may be…it is not of God.

You may say, "After all, isn't this a new age? So this must really be something that is advanced insight on how I can find my destiny, my future." Don't believe it!

I am not talking about people going to some parlor on a side street where they go into a darkened room. In the room there is a witch-like person with a hooked nose leaning over a crystal ball. This person draws their black drapes and brings you in, then smiles at you with jagged teeth that look green at the roots and says, "Come, and I'll tell you about your future."

Rather, psychic counselors are very, very attractively packaged. They are intelligent, sensitive, and gifted people. They may step onto the television set and say, "You know, we live in a day when people need the counsel they can get by their own wisdom, and if you'll call the psychic counsel line...." And then there's the number—$3.95, $4.95 for the first five minutes, $1.95 thereafter or whatever it may be—and you can get all the counsel you want.

My dear friend, as attractive as a psychic counselor may seem, you are in fact dealing with the witch of Endor. Her cave isn't a place to which you must travel. Her cave may be a television set in your own home. And it's not done in some nook or cranny in a dimly-lit corner of town or a highway stop where someone says, "Come and let me read your palm and I'll tell you your future." The adversary now presents himself with slyness and stealth as he camouflages his true intent of deception.

THE
ANGEL
OF
"I AM"

The angel of "I am" is a kind of mind science. Why is "I am, and there is none beside me" a giving over to evil? To begin with, God alone is the One who has claimed the term "I AM" as title for Himself. It is one thing to say, "I am tired." It is another thing to say, "I AM." Because when Moses stood before the Lord and said, *"When I come to the children of Israel and say to them, 'The God of your fathers has sent me to you,' and they say to me, 'What is His name?' what shall I say?"* The Lord answered Moses, *"I AM WHO I AM…you shall say to the children of Israel, I AM has sent me to you"* (Exodus 3:13-14).

God's "I AM" means two things. First, it is God's way of saying in simplest terms, "I AM eternally existent. I always have been. There was never a moment that I did not exist. I always shall be. There will never be a time I will not be, and I AM presently. I AM. I AM all existent" It is important that we do not confuse the word "existent" with "existence." God is not all existence, for all things we call existence, He created. But God is forever existent. Secondly, "I AM" is a statement of God's power—His full sufficiency. He states unequivocally that there is not one besides Him. He alone is qualified to say, "I AM."

The Bible warns against the danger of saying, "I am. No one is going to tell me what to do. I've got my own smarts and stuff. And I'm going to do it my way."

A couple of decades ago, there was a ballad which said, "When it's all over I'm just going to stand there and say, *I did it my way.*" There is something in us that resonates to those words and says, "Boy, that's gutsy! That's got the moxie that I'd like to have in my life!" I'm not suggesting that God has called people to wimp out in order to prove they trust in Him. I am saying that when people come to the place where they say, "I am, and there is none besides me," they are playing into the hands of the original fallen angel, Lucifer, who said, "I will be like the most High. I will be 'I am.'" And Lucifer was cast out, and the host of fallen angels who chose to follow in his party were cast out as well. Today these fallen angels traffic in their same program of pride. They seduce people with any number of philosophic systems that very subtly waltz around the issue of truth and veil it in notions of human adequacy without God.

This can even be said in ennobling ways. People say, "There may be a God, but He is a cosmic force that is kind of present everywhere and you just tap into it. Really, it is more or less you—your own essence." And as people fall: "Well, yeah, I believe in God, but He is basically sort of everywhere." These ideas are pantheistic. Pantheism is as old as humanity. That is because when humankind (Adam and Eve) first arrived on the scene, Satan had already started this program. It is the whole program of angelic self-sufficiency. It is spawned in hell, and it is ministered by demons to whom people submit themselves when they buy into that philosophic system at any level. This exists in any number of religious traditions. It also exists in people having no religious relationship, who nonetheless say, "This is what I believe and how I'll live."

THE
ANGEL
OF
PSYCHIC
COUNSEL

I want to discuss how psychic counsel works, and why it sometimes seems to work. There are many terms used to describe mediums: witches, psychic-type counselors, enchanters, sorcerers, diviners, and soothsayers. These are terms which have existed throughout history in all languages, and these are terms in our own language, as well. Most of them sound a little archaic except for the more recent term, "psychic counselor." But it's all of the same genre. It's all the same cut of cloth.

What does a psychic counselor do? A psychic counselor or a medium is a person whom the Bible refers to as having a "familiar spirit." Let me define "familiar spirit." This is out of the current edition of *Webster's Dictionary,* a "familiar spirit" is defined as: "A spirit or demon who serves or prompts an individual or medium to advise or prophesy."

Most psychic counselors will explain that they draw their power from some kind of energy they have tapped into—some kind of spiritual pipeline, some kind of being. Some will even name the counselor or the angel who is their source of counsel, which in reality is a demon who is a familiar spirit.

A familiar spirit is a spirit who traffics in relationship with any number of other demons at any time. It has the power, under the satanic order of things, to call for other spirits. Sometimes, it wants to deceive people into thinking it is the human spirit of someone who has died. The truth of the matter is, people who have died are gone. What is speaking through these mediums is *not* a departed loved one. It's a fallen angel masquerading as a human spirit. These fallen angels are everywhere and can travel at the speed of thought. They can be there at a moment's notice. A familiar spirit can call for the demon who has any information it needs pertaining to the person with whom the medium is conversing. That is why oftentimes the deceptive information given seems valid—because it is so accurate.

There are several terms used to describe the

word familiar:

1) relating to a family,
2) acquainted with history,
3) knowledgeable regarding personal traits, and
4) moderately tame.

Let's probe the third of these terms as we study how a familiar spirit works: knowledgeable regarding personal traits.

Let's suppose that someone's mother had died and he wanted to contact her. Let's say the man was either grieving or just wanting other information, so he contacted a psychic counselor. In order to gain credence, the counselor says, "Your mother died just eighteen months ago, didn't she?" Astonished, the person would concede that the psychic was right.

How does a psychic counselor know? They know because there are demon spirits that furnish them this information. These spirits are aware of family information, even if the family had nothing to do with demons. But demons see things and know things. Also, they are incredibly wise and intelligent. All angelic beings are stronger and smarter than we are—they're on another wavelength in terms of plain intelligence and have another resource in terms of power. They're supernatural in both areas. They don't even begin to approach or compare to the power of God, the wisdom of God, or the knowledge of God; but they have more intelligence and knowledge than we do. It is as if they use huge computer banks which transcend anything we have. And they can call upon the information and feed it in through the psychic counselor or the familiar spirit.

They could tell you any number of things. "Well, your mother died eighteen months ago. Your mother's favorite color was…" And you say, "That's right. I can trust this person. They really are in touch. How did you know this?" Finally, when you have enough things from the statements about the nature of your problem, the psychic counselors say, "I sense that you…" Yes, they do sense these things. They sense them by a supernatural power. Why? A psychic counselor has submitted himself or herself to a fallen angel who gives him or her this information. The fallen angel can draw on any number of sources who are aware just by their presence around your circumstance or the circumstances of others. The familiar spirit traffics in contact with other demon beings. That's why it works. And it becomes very convincing, very persuasive. Ultimately, the hook sinks into the person, then the person begins to sink himself and is dragged down into this system.

Dear friend, please hear me. You can submit to this kind of thing for a lifetime and even succeed for a while. But the day will come when the angel to which you have submitted will unmask itself, and behind the mask you will find the hideousness of a demon from hell. A demon who has sought to seize your soul so that you might be damned eternally. Hence, the glorious purpose of the living God for you may never be realized!

THE
ANGEL
OF
THE
STARS
(ASTROLOGICAL ANGEL)

When we come to the matter of the stargazing—the angel of the stars—the same thing is true. Scientifically speaking, horoscopes are probably the most ludicrous proposition that exists in the realm of the occult. A horoscope is based on "scoping" or seeing the hour (horos, horoscope) of your birth and the placement of the stars at the moment you were born on earth. A stargazer or astrologer will tell a person: "The cosmic energies that intersected you at that exact moment of your birth set the course for your life as a child of the cosmos. From that moment, there has been a direction for you to follow, and I will show you that direction."

To begin with (just to argue from an intellectual standpoint) the charts they use reach back four thousand years. If this actually has to do with anything from the stars, the charts would be invalid today because the position of the stars has changed sufficiently, though slightly. (But that's quite an aside.) The most important issue is what God says in His Word.

What is happening when a person submits himself to the whole system of the horoscope—to the monthly prognosticators? Some people say, "Well, it's just a curiosity, I just do this for fun. It's not really a big thing with me." You may do that just as an adventure for a start, and that's the way the bait is offered at first. But as you finally bite into that bait, the day will come when the hook will sink in. There are people reading this book who know better than to mess around curiously with horoscope matters. You say, "Well, it's just what's in the daily paper. I don't seek a psychic counselor." But psychic counselors write the stuff that's in the daily paper. People who have submitted themselves to demon beings do that. That isn't something that came out of a friendly user handbook for people who want horoscopes but not demons. That kind of thing doesn't exist. This is something cut out of the cloth of darkness.

People say, "What sign are you born under?"

I'm going to tell you—if you're a believer in Jesus Christ—it doesn't make any difference what sign you were born under because it doesn't control your destiny. If you are a believer and somebody asks you that, tell them the sign you were *reborn* under—say, "I was born under the sign of the cross." And when you get under that sign, that's another realm. There is a real power from the cross of Jesus Christ—but that's not a power out of the stars.

Why do demons function from out of the stars? What do the stars have to do with it, anyway? I'll tell you my deep personal conviction about how I believe the stars got involved in this to begin with. The Bible says that Lucifer was cast down and a third part of the heavenly beings followed him and became fallen angels or demonic beings (Revelation 12:5; Isaiah 4:12-15). The Bible calls them a third of the stars. I believe that's an inference, not just a poetic figure alone. I think it's an inference to the fact that all beings in God's creation have purpose, and probably those angelic beings, before they fell, had administrative roles throughout the cosmos. God created them, and they had roles and duties in different parts of the heavenlies. Although, I don't know what those roles or responsibilities would have been. When they lost their place or office, and were cast down like a den of snakes into the earth to ply their evil, they still longed for their former glory. Unable to have their former glory, they'll snake their arm around a person's shoulder and say, "Just look to the sky for your directions." But the energy isn't coming from the sky. The energy is coming from that dark being who seeks to control. And even if it's just for a moment, the demon hopes to recover some sense of glory: he does this by getting the person (through control) to look at the sky and what was his former glory and privilege under God's order.

A DIVINE INSIGHT REVEALING THE NEED FOR TRUTH

In the face of these things there is a need for us to come to divine insight. We're talking about the need for truth. Look at Romans 6:16: *"Do you not know that to whom you present yourselves slaves to obey, you are that one's slaves whom you obey, whether of sin leading to death or of obedience leading to righteousness?"* Submission to sin is not necessarily an action where a person bows the knee and says, "I will." It's where a person comes to a place where he allows himself to be exposed to it.

This exposure may seem innocuous at first. Maybe everybody in the group is doing it! There are people who just go along for the ride in all kinds of things—a Ouija Board excursion at a teenage Halloween party you attended where somebody read palms or cast horoscopes or talked about your future. You may say that you had just come along for the ride, but in reality, what you did was to submit yourself to a liability. You may not have recognized the intensity or the potential long-term impact on you. I'm not talking here about people who make a calculated commitment to ongoing sin. I'm talking about people who open a door to evil which leaves them vulnerable to its long-term destructive effects.

People continue to be vulnerable, too, by failing to submit to righteousness. In Acts 19 we learn that when Paul came into Ephesus—a fountainhead for this kind of paganism—he preached the Gospel; people came to Christ. The Bible here outlines three steps these people took…indicating that they were learning how to submit to God and His righteousness. If we have failed to submit ourselves to God, the pattern followed by the people in Acts 19 can help us learn how to submit to His righteousness.

The first thing these people did was to confess their sins, whether done in ignorance or not. Well, you ask, "If I didn't mean to do it, is it still sin?" Yes, it is! Sin isn't just an action of conscious, willful rebellion. Sin is oftentimes an action of ignorance. There are sins of ignorance, but they're no less destructive. I can jump off a building and kill myself, or I can walk off the top of one in the darkness, not knowing the edge of the building is there—but I'm still just as dead when I hit bottom. People in blindness walk in the darkness, and there are probably more lives destroyed unwittingly by ignorance than by conscious rebellion.

The second thing the people at Ephesus did was to surrender all the objects that had been a part of their past involvement. There was a great burning of the books of occult literature and the objects that had been a part of their tradition.

There are people reading this book who have come to Jesus Christ. You live for Christ, yet you still tolerate cultish objects in your home and have probably never thought of it until now. Maybe you've entertained it as though it didn't really make any difference. You may be saying, "You know, that object—it was so very special to my father. I know it's kind of cultish, but it was special to my dad."

Dear loved one, please hear me. If it was special to your dad, it may have been special to him because he was bound by something that had to do with it. It might have been special to him for the wrong reasons. And there can be any number of things—artifacts, literature, books, music—which need to be taken out and burned. The Bible shows that such action is a pathway, not only of the confession of sin, but also of renunciation.

The third thing that needs to be done is to let the Lord release His power in your life. Acts 19:20 says that when the people repented and renounced those things, the Word of the Lord grew mightily and prevailed. When the Word begins to work, the power of Jesus' Blood brings deliverance and freedom. This is the insight that brings the full release of God's grace—the truth that makes you free!

A
DIVINE
CALL
TO
HONEST
SEEKERS
OF
TRUTH

I want to tell you a story about some men who lived in the Middle East. They had come by some literature from a group of people who had been brought in as slaves to their area. The literature said there is going to be a great ruler of peace that will one day be born in a certain land to a certain people. After reading the literature, they thought, "We would like to go and see this person, since this sign of a certain star evidences that his time has come."

This is the story of the Wise Men found in

Matthew 2:1-12. They lived in ancient Persia, and they were astrologers who studied the stars. They had come across the literature of Jews who had been brought in as captives some centuries before. They had found the Scriptures which read, *"A Star shall come out of Jacob"* (Numbers 24:17) *"…and then shall come Shiloh—the one who brings peace* (Genesis 49:10). And the Wise Men said, "Maybe this is the answer. Maybe this is the peace giver." So they set out on a journey.

They were men who were searching for truth, but they were searching in the wrong place. When they came to Jerusalem they said, *"Where is he who has been born King of the Jews? For we have seen His star in the East and have come to worship Him."* (Matthew 2:2). You may say, "Wasn't that information from the stars?" No—it was information from the Bible. The Bible said there would be a special star. "Well, but they were astrologers." Yes, they were; but they were also hungry for reality and for truth.

God in His mercy superintended the Wise Men's situation. They got to the wrong place— Jerusalem. The people in Jerusalem said, "You're in the wrong place. Let us show you the right place." They opened Micah 5:2 and read, *"But, you Bethlehem Ephrathah, Though you are little among the thousands of Judah, Yet out of you shall*

come forth to Me The One to be Ruler in Israel.”
And the men started down the pathway to the crib in Bethlehem, and that's where they found the Savior.

You may say, "Doesn't it say a star led them?" Yes it does…but it's an unusual star. This star was different from all of the other stars the Wise Men saw in the sky: the Bible says that this Star came and rested right over the house. What were they seeing? *They were seeing an angel from God*, an angel from God who saw earnest hearts that genuinely wanted the real thing but didn't know how to find it.

In summary, the Wise Men were honest seekers of truth who received a divine call. How did they respond?
1. They sought in the darkness.
2. They searched in the wrong place.
3. They found light in God's Word.
4. They found Christ through that light.
That's the pathway of a divine call to honest seekers of truth.

For those who know the Lord, there's plenty to learn today, plenty to understand, and a need to move in wisdom. But there are people who need the Lord: people who need to turn from "I am, and there is none besides me. I don't need a thing. I will control my own destiny." The whole

system of human pride and self plays to that—
and you can't even guarantee you're going to get
up tomorrow morning. It's the ludicrous proposition that fallen angels will try to sell you on.

THE
CALL
TO
JESUS

There is a living God who calls us to His Son Jesus Christ. When Jesus came, an angel from God said, *"For there is born to you this day in the city of David a Savior, who is Christ the Lord"* (Luke 2:11).

Jesus, as He lived out His role as Savior, came to destroy all the works of the devil. In 1 John 3:8 it says, *"...the Son of God was manifested, that He might destroy the works of the devil."* That's what Jesus is doing. Any place that hell makes inroads—in our lives, our homes, our thoughts, our habits, our practice—**Jesus comes to break that power and to set us free. By His cross and His resurrection, He distinguishes Himself as Lord above all.**

As you grow in your relationship with Jesus

Christ, you will find that the Bible is the true source of God's peace and guidance for your life. Read it often, for it is the ultimate "Source-book" for life. You do not need to seek an angel because God is there to take care of you. Know that God's holy angels are there, too, as part of His plan to minister to you, the sons and daughters of the True King, Jesus Christ.

Study Notes

Study Notes

Additional Ministry Resources

YOU AND YOUR ANGELS

This series of three messages teaches on the biblical reality of angels. Dr. Jack Hayford gives examples of angels sent by God to bring messages of His divine intent. This resource provides the believer with a sound theology and a biblical frame of reference on angels. Titles include:

> Angel Balk: Angels in WHICH Field?
> Angel Talk: Listen to WHICH Angel?
> Angel Walk: WHICH Angel to Follow?

Audio • SC-517
Video • YYAVS

WHEN GOOD ANGELS TALK

This pamphlet outlines four biblical accounts of angelic visitations to real people. The messages these good angels conveyed are sources of promise and application for us today. **WGAT**

KINGDOM WARFARE:
Prayer, Spiritual Warfare, and the Ministry of Angels

This 158-page Bible-centered study guide written and edited by Dr. Jack Hayford and his son, Mark, introduces you to the key principles essential to effective spiritual warfare today. Study practical patterns of prayer; how the role of angels is still manifest today; and how to overthrow contemporary works of darkness through prayer and through the power of: the Word, the Cross, and the Name of Jesus. Gain an important understanding of *prayer, spiritual warfare, and the ministry of angels* while learning how to apply these key themes to your daily life. **SGWA**

POWER FAITH

This book will help you discover what the Scriptures say about faith in the context of healing, miracles, restoration, salvation, prosperity, and suffering. *Power Faith* was written by Roy Hicks, Jr., former Vice President and Missions Director for the International Church of the Foursquare Gospel and the composer of the worship song, "Praise the Name of Jesus." Dr. Hicks completed this manuscript one month before his death. His life testifies to the power of active faith in reaching thousands in the name of Christ. *Power Faith*, a practical 158-page study guide, offers a dynamic and yet balanced approach to understanding the power of biblical faith and how you can find the full assurance of faith in your own Christian walk.   **SGPF**

FOCUSING ON THE FUTURE
Key Prophecies and Practical Living

Focusing on the Future is a study that will show you why prophecy is important to you and how to hear what God is saying to His people today. You'll develop a clearer understanding of how God uses prophecy to show you more about Jesus and to help you in practical, day-to-day living.   **SGFF**

AUDIO CASSETTES

867	Genesis 6-8
3236	Angels: Spirit Guides or God's Messengers? Pt.1
3239	Angels: Spirit Guides or God's Messengers? Pt.2
3254	Angels: Spirit Guides or God's Messengers? Pt.3
3284	Heaven's "Quick Strike" Force
3874	Our Invisible Means of Support

ORDER FORM

Qty.	Item	Code	Price	Total
____	_____	____	____	____
____	_____	____	____	____
____	_____	____	____	____
____	_____	____	____	____
____	_____	____	____	____
____	_____	____	____	____
____	_____	____	____	____
____	_____	____	____	____
____	_____	____	____	____
____	_____	____	____	____

Postage and Handling

$0.00 - $9.99 . . . . $3.00
$10.00 - $29.99 . . . . $5.00
$30.00 - $59.99 . . . . $7.00
$60.00 and up . . . . Free Shipping
All orders outside the USA . . $5. min,
or 20% of Subtotal

Subtotal _____

Add 8.25% sales tax to CA orders _____

Shipping and Handling _____

Donation (Optional) _____

Total _____

Name _____

Street Address _____

City _____ State _____ Zip _____

Phone Number (_____) _____

Method of Payment: ❑ Check or Money Order ❑ Visa ❑ MC

_____ / _____-_____-_____-_____ / _____
Signature   Card Number   Exp. Date

RESOURCES

LIVING·WAY MINISTRIES

14820 Sherman Way, Van Nuys, CA 91405-2233

Please call for prices and ordering information:
1-800-776-8180 • 1-818-779-8480

Please include your remittance (U.S. currency only) with order.
Make check or money order payable to Living Way Ministries.